a gift for:

_____

May the God of hope fill you with
all joy and peace as you trust in him,
so that you may overflow with hope
by the power of the Holy Spirit.

ROMANS 15:13

from:

_____

ZONDERVAN®

Footprints: Scripture with Reflections Inspired by the Best-Loved Poem

Copyright © 2000 by Margaret Fishback Powers

Requests for information should be addressed to:
Zondervan, *Grand Rapids, Michigan 49530*

ISBN 978-0-310-33987-8

Excerpts taken from: *The Footprints Book of Prayer*. Copyright © 1996 by Margaret Fishback Powers; *Life's Little Instruction Book II*. Copyright © 1995 by Margaret Fishback Powers. *Footprints*. Copyright © 1996 by Margaret Fishback Powers.

All Scripture quotations, unless otherwise indicated, are taken from The Holy Bible, *New International Version®, NIV®*. Copyright © 1973, 1978, 1984, Biblica, Inc.™ Used by permission. All rights reserved worldwide.

The poem "Footprints" is © 1964 by Margaret Fishback Powers. All rights reserved. Published by arrangement with HarperCollins Publishers Ltd, Toronto, Canada.

Cover design: Gearbox
Cover photography: f9photos / Shutterstock
Interior illustration: Images © Shutterstock: pages i, iii-vi, 2-6, 8-13, 15-17, 19-20, 22, 24-27, 29-32, 34-40, 43-62, 64-75, 77-78, 80-88, 90-97, 99-109, 111-117, 119-153, 155-160, 162, 164-171, 173-178, 180-186.
Interior design: Mallory Perkins

Printed in China

14 15 16 17 18 19 20 LEO 21 20 19 18 17 16 15 14 13 12 11 10 9 8 7 6 5 4 3 2

FOOTPRINTS

SCRIPTURE WITH REFLECTIONS
INSPIRED BY THE BEST-LOVED POEM

by Margaret Fishback Powers

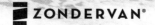

Footprints

One right I dreamed a dream.
I was walking along the beach with my Lord.
Across the dark sky flashed scenes from my life.
For each scene, I noticed two sets of footprints in the sand,
one belonging to me and one to my Lord.
When the last scene of my life shot before me
I looked back at the footprints in the sand
and to my surprise,
I noticed that many times along the path of my life
there was only one set of footprints.
I realized that this was at the lowest
and saddest times of my life.
This always bothered me
and I questioned the Lord about my dilemma.
"Lord, you told me when I decided to follow You,
You would walk and talk with me all the way.
But I'm aware that during the most troublesome
times of my life there is only one set of footprints.
I just don't understand why, when I needed You most,
You leave me."
He whispered, "My precious child,
I love you and will never leave you
never, ever, during your trials and testings.
When you saw only one set of footprints
it was then that I carried you."

Contents

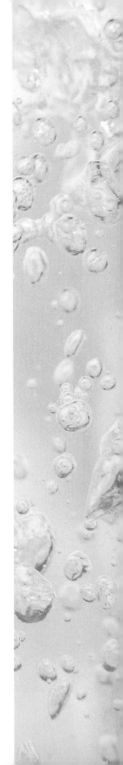

Preface

Every now and then during our devotional time my husband, Paul and I reread the poem I wrote for him back in 1964. During these times of renewal and prayer, we talk over the events of our lives and share burdens we have for ourselves and others. Very often, we realize that the Great Shepherd has once again reached out and carried us through the day as we spend these introspective moments together.

If the pleasure of sharing these thoughts anew has taught us anything, it is this: that God's word is true. Our Heavenly Father is faithful and will never leave us or forsake us. As we come to him daily, willing to be shaped and directed, his Word gives guideposts of clear direction. Almost everything we read, see, and experience shows us in some way that, although we do not visibly see God, he is with us. Over centuries of time others have looked back to understand that God's Spirit and presence were there, even when they felt alone.

In our quiet moments of reflection, in the fellowship of others, and evening dreams, God opens the doors to our hearts. This is what happened when I originally wrote the poem, "Footprints."

After hours of wrestling with the darkness of doubt and despair, I finally surrendered to him and, in the early morning light of peace, wrote the poem as result of that spiritual experience.

Listen for the gentle stirring of God's grace in your own mind and soul as you read these verses of encouragement. Each of us is different in our spiritual need, just as each day, reflecting on his Word, it will help you to know Him better.

Spiritual growth is not so much what we have done, but the feeling of love for him we put into everything we do. It is not so much in knowing about God that we grow, but in getting to know him in a personal, relational way. It is in becoming "a friend of God" as Abraham did that we grow in his grace, talking with him as our companion along the way, and letting God sift our thoughts and plans through the standards of his word. May these verses encourage you anew each day as you walk with him.

—Margaret Fishback Powers

ONE NIGHT
I dreamed a dream.

God

is with us . . .

In Our Dreams

Some of our dreams can have a powerful effect on us. All of us have, at one time or another, awakened laughing or fretful—and all because of a dream. The Bible tells us about many people who had dreams and visions that were given to them by God . . .

*[Jacob] had a dream in which he saw a stairway resting on
the earth, with its top reaching to heaven, and the angels of
God were ascending and descending on it.*

∿ G<small>ENESIS</small> 28:12

*Joseph had a dream, and when he told it to his brothers, they
hated him all the more.*

∿ G<small>ENESIS</small> 37:5

*At Gibeon the L<small>ORD</small> appeared to Solomon during the night
in a dream, and God said, "Ask for whatever you want me to
give you."*

∿ 1 K<small>INGS</small> 3:5

*An angel of the Lord appeared to Joseph in a dream. "Get up,"
he said, "take the child and his mother and escape to Egypt.
Stay there until I tell you, for Herod is going to search for the
child to kill him."*

∿ M<small>ATTHEW</small> 2:13

*After Herod died, an angel of the Lord appeared in a dream
to Joseph in Egypt and said, "Get up, take the child and his
mother and go to the land of Israel, for those who were trying
to take the child's life are dead."*

∿ M<small>ATTHEW</small> 2:19–20

*One day at about three in the afternoon [Cornelius] had a
vision. He distinctly saw an angel of God, who came to him
and said, "Cornelius!"*

∿ A<small>CTS</small> 10:3

During the night Paul had a vision of a man of Macedonia standing and begging him, "Come over to Macedonia and help us."

⌒ Acts 16:9

Some of our dreams are disappointing, but these are "wishful thinking" dreams, things we come up with in our own minds, circumstances or situations that we wish would happen. Only a small portion of these kinds of dreams ever come true. In fact, these dreams can be harmful if we allow them to fill us with false hope . . .

This is what the LORD Almighty says:

"Do not listen to what the prophets are prophesying to you;
they fill you with false hopes.
They speak visions from their own minds,
not from the mouth of the LORD."

⌒ JEREMIAH 23:16

Yet we should not ignore our dreams. God will sometimes use our dreams to assure us of his promises or to tell us something about himself. And when God does speak to us in dreams, he will also help us understand them . . .

God said, "Listen to my words:

"When a prophet of the LORD is among you,
I reveal myself to him in visions,
I speak to him in dreams."

⌒ NUMBERS 12:6

I will pour out my Spirit on all people.
Your sons and daughters will prophesy,
your old men will dream dreams,
your young men will see visions.

⌒ JOEL 2:28

Jesus left his disciples with a great promise that is true for us today: "Surely I am with you always, to the very end of the age" (Matthew 28:20).

God's presence with us is a reality. Acts 2:17 also tells us that God will pour his "Spirit on all people." As we dream our dreams with the knowledge that God is with us, we will begin to see things as Christ does and dream dreams inspired by the Holy Spirit that are worth retelling and following.

I WAS WALKING
along the beach with my Lord.

God

is with us . . .

In Our Daily Walk

God will teach us his ways,
so that we may walk in his paths.

                ISAIAH 2:3

May God turn our hearts to him, to walk in all his ways and
to keep the commands, decrees and regulations he gave our
fathers.

                1 KINGS 8:58

Your love is ever before me, Lord,
and I walk continually in your truth.

                PSALM 26:3

Walk in the way of understanding.

                PROVERBS 9:6

He whose walk is upright fears the LORD.

                PROVERBS 14:2

The ways of the LORD are right;
the righteous walk in them.

                HOSEA 14:9

He whose walk is blameless is kept safe.

                PROVERBS 28:18

Let us walk in the light of the LORD.

                ISAIAH 2:5

Whether you turn to the right or to the left, your ears will hear a voice behind you, saying, "This is the way; walk in it."

        ᴄ~ ISAIAH 30:21

The Bible tells us that maintaining a close walk with God is a command we must obey, not merely a suggestion we may want to consider.

I am God Almighty; walk before me and be blameless.

        ᴄ~ GENESIS 17:1

What does the LORD your God ask of you but to fear the LORD your God, to walk in all his ways, to love him, to serve the LORD your God with all your heart and with all your soul.

        ᴄ~ DEUTERONOMY 10:12

*Love the LORD your God . . . walk in all his ways . . . hold
fast to him.*

> ⌒ DEUTERONOMY 11:22

*The LORD will establish you . . . if you keep the commands of
the Lord your God and walk in his ways.*

> ⌒ DEUTERONOMY 28:9

*God has showed you, O man, what is good.
And what does the LORD require of you?
To act justly and to love mercy
and to walk humbly with your God.*

> ⌒ MICAH 6:8

*This is love: that we walk in obedience to God's commands.
As you have heard from the beginning, his command is that
you walk in love.*

> ⌒ 2 JOHN 6

*Obey me, and I will be your God and you will be my people.
Walk in all the ways I command you, that it may go well
with you.*

> ⌒ JEREMIAH 7:23

*Be very careful to keep the commandment and the law that
Moses the servant of the LORD gave you: to love the LORD
your God, to walk in all his ways, to obey his commands, to
hold fast to him and to serve him with all your heart and all
your soul.*

> ⌒ JOSHUA 22:5

But what does a walk with God actually entail? How does God want us to live?

> Love the LORD your God with all your heart and with all your soul and with all your strength. These commandments that I give you today are to be upon your hearts. Impress them on your children. Talk about them when you sit at home and when you walk along the road, when you lie down and when you get up.
>
> ⌒ DEUTERONOMY 6:5–7

> He whose walk is blameless
> and who does what is righteous,
> who speaks the truth from his heart
> and has no slander on his tongue,
> who does his neighbor no wrong
> and casts no slur on his fellowman,
> who despises a vile man
> but honors those who fear the LORD,
> who keeps his oath
> even when it hurts,
> who lends his money without usury
> and does not accept a bribe against the innocent.
> He who does these things
> will never be shaken.
>
> ⌒ PSALM 15:2–5

Many of these things that God asks us to do go against our nature. Yet Nehemiah asks us "Shouldn't you walk in the fear of our God to avoid . . . reproach?" (Nehemiah 5:9). The Bible urges us to consistently walk with the Lord, walking by faith, even when it's difficult.

Live a life worthy of the Lord . . . please him in every way: bearing fruit in every good work, growing in the knowledge of God.

                            COLOSSIANS 1:10

Just as you received Christ Jesus as Lord, continue to live in him.

                            COLOSSIANS 2:6

If we walk in the light, as he is in the light, we have fellowship with one another, and the blood of Jesus, his Son, purifies us from all sin.

                            1 JOHN 1:7

Whoever claims to live in God must walk as Jesus did.

                            1 JOHN 2:6

We live by faith, not by sight.

                            2 CORINTHIANS 5:7

Jesus said, "Walk while you have the light, before darkness overtakes you. The man who walks in the dark does not know where he is going. Put your trust in the light while you have it, so that you may become sons of light."

                            JOHN 12:35–36

Live a life of love, just as Christ loved us.

                            EPHESIANS 5:2

Health professionals suggest that people who want to become physically fit should try a consistent program of walking. Sustained walking several times a week will improve your muscle tone and strengthen your heart.

The Bible reassures us that our spiritual lives will also reap benefits when we are consistent in walking with the Lord. Look at the many benefits a walk with God provides . . .

Walk in all the way that the LORD your God has commanded you, so that you may live and prosper and prolong your days in the land that you will possess.

                                       DEUTERONOMY 5:33

I will walk among you and be your God, and you will be my people.

                                       LEVITICUS 26:12

I command you today to love the LORD your God, to walk in his ways, and to keep his commands, decrees and laws; then you will live and increase, and the LORD your God will bless you.

                                       DEUTERONOMY 30:16

Observe what the LORD your God requires: Walk in his ways . . . so that you may prosper in all you do and wherever you go.

                                       1 KINGS 2:3

If you walk in my ways and obey my statutes and commands . . . I will give you a long life.

                                       1 KINGS 3:14

If you do whatever I command you and walk in my ways and do what is right in my eyes by keeping my statutes and commands . . . I will be with you.

                                       1 KINGS 11:38

The LORD God is a sun and shield;
the LORD bestows favor and honor;
no good thing does he withhold
from those whose walk is blameless.

C∼ PSALM 84:11

Blessed are they whose ways are blameless,
who walk according to the law of the LORD.
Blessed are they who keep his statutes
and seek him with all their heart.
They do nothing wrong;
they walk in his ways.

C∼ PSALM 119:1–3

Blessed are all who fear the LORD,
who walk in his ways.
You will eat the fruit of your labor;
blessings and prosperity will be yours.

C∼ PSALM 128:1–2

I guide you in the way of wisdom
and lead you along straight paths
When you walk, your steps will not be hampered;
when you run, you will not stumble.

C∼ PROVERBS 4:11–12

Those who hope in the LORD
will renew their strength.
They will soar on wings like eagles;
they will run and not grow weary,
they will walk and not be faint.

C∼ ISAIAH 40:31

He is a shield to those whose walk is blameless.

C∼ PROVERBS 2:7

We are the temple of the living God. As God has said: "I will
live with them and walk among them, and I will be their
God, and they will be my people."

↬ 2 Corinthians 6:16

Blessed is the man
who does not walk in the counsel of the wicked
or stand in the way of sinners
or sit in the seat of mockers.
But his delight is in the law of the Lord,
and on his law he meditates day and night.
He is like a tree planted by streams of water,
which yields its fruit in season
and whose leaf does not wither.
Whatever he does prospers.

↬ Psalm 1:1–3

This is what the Lord says:
"Stand at the crossroads and look;
ask for the ancient paths,
ask where the good way is, and walk in it,
and you will find rest for your souls."

↬ Jeremiah 6:16

Fanny Crosby once said that the Lord "lovingly guards my footsteps and gives me songs in the night." A joyful heart is the mark of one who has a consistent walk with the Lord, who follows in the footsteps of the Master.

Take strength then, and be blessed in a close walk with the Lord, for "I will strengthen them in the Lord and in his name they will walk," declares the Lord (Zechariah 10:12).

ACROSS THE DARK SKY
flashed scenes from my life.

God
is with us . . .

In the Hard Times

We all go through times when life seems to overwhelm us. The Bible reassures us that God's presence is with us to help us, even when we don't realize it.

God is our refuge and strength,
an ever-present help in trouble.

~ PSALM 46:1

In my distress I called to the LORD,
and he answered me.
I called for help,
and you listened to my cry.

~ JONAH 2:2

You are my hiding place;
you will protect me from trouble
and surround me with songs of deliverance.

~ PSALM 32:7

Even though I walk
through the valley of the shadow of death,
I will fear no evil,
for you are with me;
your rod and your staff,
they comfort me.

~ PSALM 23:4

Praise be to the Lord, to God our Savior,
who daily bears our burdens.

~ PSALM 68:19

My soul finds rest in God alone;
my salvation comes from him.
He alone is my rock and my salvation;
he is my fortress, I will never be shaken.

~ PSALM 62:1–2

The LORD is my strength and my shield;
my heart trusts in him, and I am helped.

—PSALM 28:7

Moments of darkness in our lives may be caused by the death of a loved one, the loss of a job or a home, or another great tragedy of life. Yet there is a greater darkness than these tragedies: the darkness in the eyes of one who has not felt God's love, grace, and the assurance of his hope. There is hope for all of us. There is light. Jesus Christ, the Son of God, is our hope and light in darkness.

*You are my lamp, O L*ORD*;*
the L*ORD *turns my darkness into light.*

↶ 2 SAMUEL 22:29

For you were once darkness, but now you are light in the
Lord. Live as children of light.

↶ EPHESIANS 5:8

You are a chosen people, a royal priesthood, a holy nation, a
people belonging to God, that you may declare the praises of
him who called you out of darkness into his wonderful light.

↶ 1 PETER 2:9

Jesus said, "I am the light of the world. Whoever follows me
will never walk in darkness, but will have the light of life."

↶ JOHN 8:12

God is light; in him there is no darkness at all. If we claim to
have fellowship with him yet walk in the darkness, we lie and
do not live by the truth. But if we walk in the light, as he is in
the light, we have fellowship with one another, and the blood
of Jesus, his Son, purifies us from all sin.

↶ 1 JOHN 1:5–7

Let him who walks in the dark,
who has no light,
trust in the name of the LORD
and rely on his God.

↶ ISAIAH 50:10

Jesus said, "I have come into the world as a light, so that no
one who believes in me should stay in darkness."

↶ JOHN 12:46

In my distress I called to the LORD;
I called out to my God.
From his temple he heard my voice;
my cry came to his ears . . .
He reached down from on high and took hold of me;
he drew me out of deep waters . . .
He brought me out into a spacious place;
he rescued me because he delighted in me.

                             ᴄ 2 SAMUEL 22:7, 17, 20

The people walking in darkness
have seen a great light;
on those living in the land of the shadow of death
a light has dawned.

                                 ᴄ ISAIAH 9:2

Darkness covers the earth
and thick darkness is over the peoples,
but the LORD rises upon you
and his glory appears over you.

                                ᴄ ISAIAH 60:2

The LORD will be your everlasting light,
and your God will be your glory.

                              ᴄ ISAIAH 60:19

Though I have fallen, I will rise.
Though I sit in darkness,
the LORD will be my light . . .
He will bring me out into the light;
I will see his righteousness.

                                ᴄ MICAH 7:8–9

Because of the tender mercy of our God . . .
the rising sun will come to us from heaven
to shine on those living in darkness
and in the shadow of death,
to guide our feet into the path of peace.

LUKE 1:78–79

Our dark times may also be times when God wants to teach us something more about ourselves and his love for us. Our faith can be strengthened if we will wait patiently and trust God's heart-desire to make us more like himself.

A righteous man may have many troubles,
but the LORD delivers him from them all.

                     ᕁ PSALM 34:19

Though you have made me see troubles, many and bitter,
you will restore my life again;
from the depths of the earth
you will again bring me up.

                     ᕁ PSALM 71:20

We must go through many hardships to enter the kingdom
of God.

                     ᕁ ACTS 14:22

Be joyful in hope, patient in affliction, faithful in prayer.

                     ᕁ ROMANS 12:12

Our light and momentary troubles are achieving for us an
eternal glory that far outweighs them all. So we fix our eyes
not on what is seen, but on what is unseen. For what is seen is
temporary, but what is unseen is eternal.

                     ᕁ 2 CORINTHIANS 4:17–18

We are hard pressed on every side, but not crushed; perplexed, but not in despair; persecuted, but not abandoned; struck down, but not destroyed . . . We who are alive are always being given over to death for Jesus' sake, so that his life may be revealed in our mortal body.

⤳ 2 CORINTHIANS 4:8–9, 11

Do not be surprised at the painful trial you are suffering, as though something strange were happening to you. But rejoice that you participate in the sufferings of Christ, so that you may be overjoyed when his glory is revealed.

⤳ 1 PETER 4:12–13

Tragedy or testing, dark days or dreary nights, God knows what we are facing. He is in touch with what is happening to us, and he is concerned.

His eyes are on the ways of men;
he sees their every step.

⤳ JOB 34:21

Though I walk in the midst of trouble,
you preserve my life . . .
with your right hand you save me.

⤳ PSALM 138:7

He knows the way that I take;
when he has tested me, I will come forth as gold.

⌒ JOB 23:10

I will be glad and rejoice in your love,
for you saw my affliction
and knew the anguish of my soul.

⌒ PSALM 31:7

You, LORD, discern my going out and my lying down;
you are familiar with all my ways.

⌒ PSALM 139:3

The LORD will keep you from all harm—
he will watch over your life;
the LORD will watch over your coming and going
both now and forevermore.

⌒ PSALM 121:7–8

When you pass through the waters,
I will be with you;
and when you pass through the rivers,
they will not sweep over you.
When you walk through the fire,
you will not be burned;
the flames will not set you ablaze.

⌒ ISAIAH 43:2

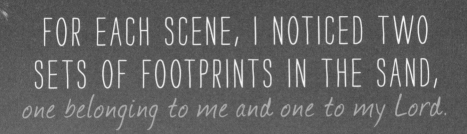

FOR EACH SCENE, I NOTICED TWO
SETS OF FOOTPRINTS IN THE SAND,
one belonging to me and one to my Lord.

God

is with us . . .

As Our Companion

I have a friend who loves to take long walks with me. We talk and laugh and enjoy each other's company as we stroll along. The exercise is beneficial, and so is the conversation.

The Lord is a lot like my friend. He enjoys walking with us as our companion on life's pathway. And he brings blessing into our lives when we walk closely with him.

> *If we walk in the light, as he is in the light, we have fellowship with one another, and the blood of Jesus, his Son, purifies us from all sin.*
>
> ⌒ 1 JOHN 1:7

> *Walk in God's ways, and keep his decrees and commands, his laws and requirements . . . so that you may prosper in all you do and wherever you go.*
>
> ⌒ 1 KINGS 2:3

Blessed are those who have learned to acclaim you,
who walk in the light of your presence, O Lord.

                     ᴄ PSALM 89:15

Walk in all the way that the Lord your God has commanded
you, so that you may live and prosper and prolong your days
in the land that you will possess.

                 ᴄ DEUTERONOMY 5:33

I will walk among you and be your God, and you will be my
people.

                   ᴄ LEVITICUS 26:12

"If you walk in my ways and obey my statutes and commands
I will give you a long life," says the Lord.

                     ᴄ 1 KINGS 3:14

Blessed are all who fear the Lord,
who walk in his ways.
You will eat the fruit of your labor;
blessings and prosperity will be yours.

                     ᴄ PSALM 128:1–2

"Walk in all the ways I command you, that it may go well
with you."

                     ᴄ JEREMIAH 7:23

We are the temple of the living God. As God has said: "I will
live with them and walk among them, and I will be their
God, and they will be my people."

                 ᴄ 2 CORINTHIANS 6:16

The Lord said, "If you do whatever I command you and walk in my ways and do what is right in my eyes by keeping my statutes and commands . . . I will be with you."

               ᴄ~ 1 Kings 11:38

Ask where the good way is, and walk in it, and you will find rest for your souls.

               ᴄ~ Jeremiah 6:16

God is a shield to those whose walk is blameless.

               ᴄ~ Proverbs 2:7

Come . . . let us walk in the light of the Lord.

               ᴄ~ Isaiah 2:5

Though I walk in the midst of trouble, you preserve my life; you stretch out your hand . . . with your right hand you save me.

               ᴄ~ Psalm 138:7

The awareness of God's presence with us is encouraging and heart-warming. It is as if we were two friends seated beside a rippling brook, enjoying a gentle breeze on a warm spring afternoon.

Jesus said, "Here I am! I stand at the door and knock. If anyone hears my voice and opens the door, I will come in and eat with him, and he with me."

               ᴄ~ Revelation 3:20

Come near to God and he will come near to you.

               ᴄ~ James 4:8

"Abraham believed God, and it was credited to him as righteousness," and he was called God's friend.

∿ JAMES 2:23

I am a friend to all who fear you,
to all who follow your precepts.

∿ PSALM 119:63

Jesus said, "You are my friends if you do what I command . . .
I have called you friends, for everything that I learned from my
Father I have made known to you. You did not choose me, but I
chose you."

∿ JOHN 15:14–16

Even when we are surrounded by family and friends, some problems seem to double in size of their own accord. If we toss and turn in the early morning hours thinking about them, they become ten times as large. Yet though it seems the whole world has gone wrong around us, we are not alone—God is with us!

So do not fear, for I am with you;
do not be dismayed, for I am your God.
I will strengthen you and help you;
I will uphold you with my righteous right hand.

∿ ISAIAH 41:10

Jesus said, "I will not leave you as orphans; I will come to you."

∿ JOHN 14:18

Jesus said, "For where two or three come together in my name, there am I with them."

The eternal God is your refuge,
and underneath are the everlasting arms.

DEUTERONOMY 33:27

Who shall separate us from the love of Christ? Shall trouble or hardship or persecution or famine or nakedness or danger or sword? . . . No, in all these things we are more than conquerors through him who loved us. For I am convinced that neither death nor life, neither angels nor demons, neither the present nor the future, nor any powers, neither height nor depth, nor anything else in all creation, will be able to separate us from the love of God that is in Christ Jesus our Lord.

ROMANS 8:35, 37–39

For the LORD your God is a merciful God; he will not abandon or destroy you or forget the covenant with your forefathers, which he confirmed to them by oath.

DEUTERONOMY 4:31

Be strong and courageous. Do not be afraid or terrified because of them, for the LORD your God goes with you; he will never leave you nor forsake you.

DEUTERONOMY 31:6

"Though the mountains be shaken
and the hills be removed,
yet my unfailing love for you will not be shaken
nor my covenant of peace be removed,"
says the LORD, who has compassion on you.

ISAIAH 54:10

God is our refuge and strength,
an ever-present help in trouble.

PSALM 46:1

"He will call upon me, and I will answer him;
I will be with him in trouble,
I will deliver him and honor him.
With long life will I satisfy him
and show him my salvation," says the LORD.

PSALM 91:15–16

You have granted him eternal blessings
and made him glad with the joy of your presence.

PSALM 21:6

Where can I go from your Spirit?
Where can I flee from God's presence?
If I go up to the heavens, you are there;
if I make my bed in the depths, you are there.
If I rise on the wings of the dawn,
if I settle on the far side of the sea,
even there your hand will guide me,
your right hand will hold me fast.

PSALM 139:7–10

How great is your goodness,
which you have stored up for those who fear you,
which you bestow in the
    sight of men
on those who take
    refuge in you.

            Psalm 31:19

He will not let your foot slip—
he who watches over you will not slumber . . .
The Lord *watches over you—*
the Lord *is your shade at your right hand;*
the sun will not harm you by day,
nor the moon by night.
The Lord *will keep you from all harm—*
he will watch over your life;
the Lord *will watch over your coming and going*
both now and forevermore.

          Psalm 121:3, 5–8

Jesus said [to his disciples], "I will come back and take you to
be with me that you also may be where I am."

           John 14:3

Jesus said, "And surely I am with you always, to the very end
of the age."

         Matthew 28:20

 Wherever we go, we cannot step outside the boundaries of God's love and care. We can have fellowship "with the Father and with his Son, Jesus Christ" wherever we are (1 John 1:3). All we need to do is trust in God's loving companionship and walk the path he has placed before us.

WHEN THE LAST SCENE OF
MY LIFE SHOT BEFORE ME

I looked back at the footprints in the sand

God

is with us . . .

Never Look Back! No Regrets!

We say that hindsight is always 20/20. Looking back is something we often do without considering the consequences. However, looking back is not recommended in the Bible. Lot was warned not to look back toward Sodom and Gomorrah . . .

> *With the coming of dawn, the angels urged Lot, saying . . .*
> *"Flee for your lives! Don't look back, and don't stop anywhere*
> *in the plain! Flee to the mountains or you will be swept*
> *away!" . . . Then the LORD rained down burning sulfur on*
> *Sodom and Gomorrah. . . . Thus he overthrew those cities*
> *and the entire plain. But Lot's wife looked back, and she*
> *became a pillar of salt.*
>
> ⌒ GENESIS 19:15, 17, 24–26

Joshua and his men attacked their enemies in the city of Ai and quickly set the city on fire. When the men of Ai looked back, disaster fell on them . . .

> *The men of Ai looked back and saw the smoke of the city*
> *rising against the sky, but they had no chance to escape in any*
> *direction, for the Israelites who had been fleeing toward the*
> *desert had turned back against their pursuers.*
>
> ⌒ JOSHUA 8:20

Even the Lord Jesus reminded his listeners of the perils of looking back . . .

> *Jesus replied, "No one who puts his hand to the plow and*
> *looks back is fit for service in the kingdom of God."*
>
> ⌒ LUKE 9:62

When we live with an attitude that looks back over our lives with regrets and "if only's" we rob ourselves of hope. We rob ourselves of the joy of God's grace.

> *"God has delivered us from such a deadly peril, and he will deliver us. On him we have set our hope that he will continue to deliver us."*
>
> ⁓ 2 CORINTHIANS 1:10

God never changes. He is the God of grace. He is the God of hope. He is the God of love who offers us a life free of regrets.

> *God is greater than our hearts, and he knows everything.*
>
> ⁓ 1 JOHN 3:20

> *From everlasting to everlasting*
> *the LORD's love is with those who fear him,*
> *and his righteousness with their children's children—*
> *with those who keep his covenant*
> *and remember to*
> * obey his precepts.*
>
> ⁓ PSALM 103:17–18

A life without regrets does not mean a life without repentance. When we sin, we must go beyond regretting and feeling sorry for our actions. We must move on to repentance by turning from our sinful ways and embracing God's forgiveness.

> *Godly sorrow brings repentance that leads to salvation and leaves no regret.*
>
> ⁓ 2 CORINTHIANS 7:10

Therefore, if anyone is in Christ, he is a new creation; the old has gone, the new has come!

∾ 2 C<small>ORINTHIANS</small> 5:17

Cleanse me with hyssop, and I will be clean;
wash me, and I will be whiter than snow . . .
Hide your face from my sins
and blot out all my iniquity.
Create in me a pure heart, O God,
and renew a steadfast spirit within me.
Do not cast me from your presence
or take your Holy Spirit from me.
Restore to me the joy of your salvation
and grant me a willing spirit, to sustain me.

∾ P<small>SALM</small> 51:7, 9–12

When we have experienced God's forgiveness, we are new creatures. We do not need to live a life of regrets, but rather we can live with a forward-looking hope of glory!

> *I do not consider myself yet to have taken hold of it. But one thing I do: Forgetting what is behind and straining toward what is ahead, I press on toward the goal to win the prize for which God has called me heavenward in Christ Jesus.*
>
> ◟ PHILIPPIANS 3:13–14

> *Let us throw off everything that hinders and the sin that so easily entangles, and let us run with perseverance the race marked out for us. Let us fix our eyes on Jesus, the author and perfecter of our faith.*
>
> ◟ HEBREWS 12:1–2

I have fought the good fight, I have finished the race, I have kept the faith. Now there is in store for me the crown of righteousness, which the Lord, the righteous Judge, will award to me on that day.

                                       ⌒ 2 TIMOTHY 4:7–8

Whenever we do look back over our lives we must do so with God's perspective—no remorse or regrets. With God's perspective, we will be able to trace his hand on our lives and see that he has swept up the bad things of life and transformed them to good, just as he promised he would. With God's perspective we will be able to live above regrets and live in God's peace and joy.

We know that in all things God works for the good of those who love him, who have been called according to his purpose.

                                       ⌒ ROMANS 8:28

Surely goodness and love will follow me
all the days of my life,
and I will dwell in the house of the LORD
forever.

                                       ⌒ PSALM 23:6

AND TO MY SURPRISE,
I noticed that many times
along the path of my life there
was only one set of footprints

God

is with us . . .

In Our Loneliness

Toddlers often face separation anxiety—a feeling of abandonment whenever their parents leave the room. Though we may be much older and wiser than little children we still feel the pain of loneliness and isolation. Both Jesus and the psalmist also knew what it was to feel alone, abandoned, forgotten . . .

> *About the ninth hour Jesus cried out in a loud voice, "Eloi, Eloi, lama sabachthani?"—which means, "My God, my God, why have you forsaken me?"*
>
> C- MATTHEW 27:46

> *Do not hide your face from me,*
> *do not turn your servant away in anger;*
> *you have been my helper.*
> *Do not reject me or forsake me,*
> *O God my Savior.*
>
> C- PSALM 27:9

> *I say to God my Rock,*
> *"Why have you forgotten me?*
> *Why must I go about mourning,*
> *oppressed by the enemy?"*
>
> C- PSALM 42:9

> *My God, my God, why have you forsaken me?*
> *Why are you so far from saving me,*
> *so far from the words of my groaning?*
>
> C- PSALM 22:1

When we feel alone and abandoned we can take comfort in God's promises to deliver us from our isolation and pain.

> *"He will call upon me, and I will answer him;*
> *I will be with him in trouble,*
> *I will deliver him and honor him.*
> *With long life will I satisfy him*
> *and show him my salvation," says the LORD.*
>
> ~ PSALM 91:15–16

> *I the LORD will answer them;*
> *I, the God of Israel, will not forsake them.*
>
> ~ ISAIAH 41:17

> *Can a mother forget the baby at her breast*
> *and have no compassion on the child she has borne?*
> *Though she may forget,*
> *I will not forget you!*
> *See, I have engraved you on the palms of my hands.*
>
> ~ ISAIAH 49:15–16

> *You are enthroned as the Holy One;*
> *you are the praise of Israel.*
> *In you our fathers put their trust;*
> *they trusted and you delivered them.*
> *They cried to you and were saved;*
> *in you they trusted and were not disappointed.*
>
> ~ PSALM 22:3–5

The LORD will not reject his people, because the LORD was
pleased to make you his own.

                                       ᴄ⟋ I SAMUEL 12:22

Do not fear, for I am with you;
do not be dismayed, for I am your God.
I will strengthen you and help you;
I will uphold you with my righteous right hand.

                                        ᴄ⟋ ISAIAH 41:10

Jesus said, "I will not leave you as orphans; I will come to you."

                                        ᴄ⟋ JOHN 14:18

God is our refuge and strength,
an ever-present help in trouble.

                                        ᴄ⟋ PSALM 46:1

The eternal God is your refuge, and underneath are the
everlasting arms.

Jesus said, "Do not let your hearts be troubled. Trust in God;
trust also in me."

C~ JOHN 14:1

"Though the mountains be shaken
and the hills be removed,
yet my unfailing love for you will not be shaken
nor my covenant of peace be removed,"
says the LORD.

C~ ISAIAH 54:10

How great is your goodness, O LORD,
which you have stored up for those who fear you,
which you bestow in the sight of men
on those who take refuge in you.
In the shelter of your presence you hide them . . .
in your dwelling you keep them safe.

C~ PSALM 31:19–20

He will not let your foot slip—
he who watches over you will not slumber . . .
The LORD *watches over you—*
the LORD *is your shade at your right hand;*
the sun will not harm you by day,
nor the moon by night.
The LORD *will keep you from all harm—*
he will watch over your life;
the LORD *will watch over your coming and going*
both now and forevermore.

C~ PSALM 121:3, 5–8

God is always with us—in our joy and in our pain, in the good times and in the bad times. His steadfast love and faithfulness are promises we can cling to, promises to bring us joy when we face loneliness.

I will be with you; I will never leave you nor forsake you.

℘ JOSHUA 1:5

And Jesus told his disciples, "And surely I am with you always, to the very end of the age."

℘ MATTHEW 28:20

The LORD your God is a merciful God; he will not abandon or destroy you.

℘ DEUTERONOMY 4:31

Be strong and courageous. Do not be afraid or terrified for the LORD your God goes with you; he will never leave you nor forsake you.

℘ DEUTERONOMY 31:6

Jesus said, "Here I am! I stand at the door and knock. If anyone hears my voice and opens the door, I will come in and eat with him, and he with me."

℘ REVELATION 3:20

Come near to God and he will come near to you.

℘ JAMES 4:8

Those who know your name will trust in you, for you, LORD, have never forsaken those who seek you.

℘ PSALM 9:10

You have . . . made him glad with the joy of your presence.

⌒ PSALM 21:6

Where can I go from your Spirit?
Where can I flee from God's presence?
If I go up to the heavens, you are there;
if I make my bed in the depths, you are there.
If I rise on the wings of the dawn,
if I settle on the far side of the sea,
even there your hand will guide me,
your right hand will hold me fast.

⌒ PSALM 139:7–10

When loneliness overtakes us, we need to remember that we are not alone. God has promised to be with us. He will never forsake us. Lean on his promises and receive his peace.

Why are you downcast, O my soul?
Why so disturbed within me?
Put your hope in God,
for I will yet praise him,
my Savior and my God.

⌒ PSALM 42:11

Who shall separate us from the love of Christ? Shall trouble
or hardship or persecution or famine or nakedness or dan-
ger or sword? . . . No, in all these things we are more than
conquerors through him who loved us. For I am convinced
that neither death nor life, neither angels nor demons, neither
the present nor the future, nor any powers, neither height nor
depth, nor anything else in all creation, will be able to sepa-
rate us from the love of God that is in Christ Jesus our Lord.

⌒ ROMANS 8:35–39

I REALIZED THAT THIS WAS AT THE LOWEST
and saddest times of my life

God
is with us . . .

In Our Sorrow

Sorrow can cause us to doubt God's plan. The psalmist cried, "Has his unfailing love vanished forever? Has his promise failed for all time? Has God forgotten to be merciful? Has he in anger withheld his compassion?" (Psalm 77:8–9). Though we may face trouble and difficulties, sadness and pain, God is still in control, and he is always with us.

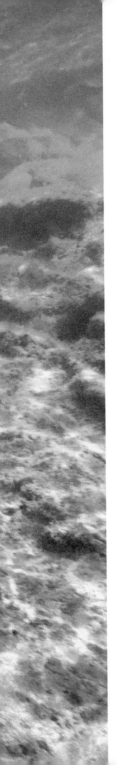

My flesh and my heart may fail,
but God is the strength of my heart
and my portion forever.

                         ᴄ᷎ PSALM 73:26

"When you pass through the waters,
I will be with you;
and when you pass through the rivers,
they will not sweep over you.
When you walk through the fire,
you will not be burned;
the flames will not set you ablaze," says the LORD.

                         ᴄ᷎ ISAIAH 43:2

When I said, "My foot is slipping,"
your love, O LORD, supported me.
When anxiety was great within me,
your consolation brought joy to my soul.

                         ᴄ᷎ PSALM 94:18–19

The LORD upholds all those who fall
and lifts up all who are bowed down.

                         ᴄ᷎ PSALM 145:14

The LORD is a refuge for the oppressed,
a stronghold in times of trouble.

                         ᴄ᷎ PSALM 9:9

The eternal God is your refuge,
and underneath are the everlasting arms.

                         ᴄ᷎ DEUTERONOMY 33:27

We must remember to listen closely to God's voice when trouble rages around us. When the agonies of life begin to crush us, God has not moved away from us. Often we have moved away from him. We need to return to him in faith and call on him for his strength.

> *I have put my trust in you.*
> *Show me the way I should go,*
> *for to you I lift up my soul.*
>
> — PSALM 143:8

> *God is our refuge and strength,*
> *an ever-present help in trouble.*
>
> — PSALM 46:1

> *He makes his steps firm;*
> *though he stumble, he will not fall,*
> *for the LORD upholds him with his hand.*
>
> — PSALM 37:23–24

> *I sought the LORD, and he answered me;*
> *he delivered me from all my fears.*
>
> — PSALM 34:4

> *A righteous man may have many troubles,*
> *but the LORD delivers him from them all.*
>
> — PSALM 34:19

> *Jesus said, "Do not let your hearts be troubled. Trust in God."*
>
> — JOHN 14:1

My soul finds rest in God alone;
my salvation comes from him.
He alone is my rock and my salvation;
he is my fortress, I will never be shaken.

ᕙ PSALM 62:1–2

Jesus said, "Peace I leave with you; my peace I give you. I do
not give to you as the world gives. Do not let your hearts be
troubled and do not be afraid."

ᕙ JOHN 14:27

Jesus told his disciples, "In this world you will have trouble.
But take heart! I have overcome the world."

ᕙ JOHN 16:33

Jesus said to me, "My grace is sufficient for you, for my power
is made perfect in weakness."

ᕙ 2 CORINTHIANS 12:9

We who have fled to take hold of the hope offered to us may
be greatly encouraged. We have this hope as an anchor for the
soul, firm and secure.

ᕙ HEBREWS 6:18–19

Praise be to the God and Father of our Lord Jesus Christ, the
Father of compassion and the God of all comfort, who com-
forts us in all our troubles, so that we can comfort those in any
trouble with the comfort we ourselves have received from God.

ᕙ 2 CORINTHIANS 1:3–4

The LORD has anointed me . . .
to comfort all who mourn, . . .
and to bestow on them a crown of beauty
instead of ashes,
the oil of gladness
instead of mourning,
and a garment of praise
instead of a spirit of despair.

ᴄ ISAIAH 61:1–3

My comfort in my suffering is this:
Your promise preserves my life, O LORD.

ᴄ PSALM 119:50

We do not have a high priest who is unable to sympathize
with our weaknesses. . . . Let us then approach the throne
of grace with confidence, so that we may receive mercy and
find grace to help us in our time of need.

ᴄ HEBREWS 4:15–16

Jesus experienced sorrow of the deepest kind in the Garden of Gethsemane—the sorrow of impending death. We also experience pain when death takes a loved one, but God reminds us that he is still in control. Death is not the master—God is.

For none of us lives to himself alone and none of us dies to
himself alone. If we live, we live to the Lord; and if we die,
we die to the Lord. So, whether we live or die, we belong to
the Lord.

ᴄ ROMANS 14:7–8

If only for this life we have hope in Christ, we are to be pitied more than all men. But Christ has indeed been raised from the dead.... Since death came through a man, the resurrection of the dead comes also through a man. For as in Adam all die, so in Christ all will be made alive.

1 CORINTHIANS 15:19–22

For to me, to live is Christ and to die is gain.

～ PHILIPPIANS 1:21

*Listen, I tell you a mystery: We will not all sleep, but we will
all be changed—in a flash, in the twinkling of an eye, at the
last trumpet. For the trumpet will sound, the dead will be
raised imperishable, and we will be changed.*

～ 1 CORINTHIANS 15:51–52

*Even though I walk
through the valley of the shadow of death,
I will fear no evil,
for you are with me;
your rod and your staff,
they comfort me.*

～ PSALM 23:4

*We believe that God will bring with Jesus those who have
fallen asleep in him . . . For the Lord himself will come down
from heaven, with a loud command, with the voice of the
archangel and with the trumpet call of God, and the dead
in Christ will rise first. After that, we who are still alive and
are left will be caught up together with them in the clouds
to meet the Lord in the air. And so we will be with the Lord
forever.*

～ 1 THESSALONIANS 4:14, 16–17

Whether we face death, discouragement, loss, or pain, we can take
great comfort in knowing that no sorrow is too deep that God cannot
feel it with us. And God wants to help deliver us from it. He wants to
bring us his divine comfort.

This I call to mind
and therefore I have hope:
Because of the LORD*'s great love we are not consumed,*
for his compassions never fail.
They are new every morning;
great is your faithfulness.

    LAMENTATIONS 3:21–23

The LORD *is good to those whose hope is in him,*
to the one who seeks him.

    LAMENTATIONS 3:25

Cast your cares on the LORD
and he will sustain you;
he will never let the righteous fall.

    PSALM 55:22

Do not be anxious about anything, but in everything,
by prayer and petition, with thanksgiving, present your
requests to God. And the peace of God, which transcends
all understanding, will guard your hearts and your minds
in Christ Jesus.

    PHILIPPIANS 4:6–7

For I am the LORD*, your God,*
who takes hold of your right hand
and says to you, "Do not fear;
I will help you."

    ISAIAH 41:13

Be strong and take heart,
all you who hope in the LORD.

⌒ PSALM 31:24

God will show compassion,
so great is his unfailing love.

⌒ LAMENTATIONS 3:32

In all their distress the LORD too was distressed,
and the angel of his presence saved them.
In his love and mercy he redeemed them;
he lifted them up and carried them.

⌒ ISAIAH 63:9

Though things may seem hopeless, "God, who has called you into fellowship with his Son Jesus Christ our Lord, is faithful" (1 Corinthians 1:9). No trial is so great that God cannot deliver us. No pain is so great that he does not bring us comfort. And no situation is ever without God's presence: "Do not fear, for I am with you; do not be dismayed, for I am your God. I will strengthen you and help you; I will uphold you with my righteous right hand" (Isaiah 41:10).

> *Jesus said, "Come to me, all you who are weary and bur-*
> *dened, and I will give you rest. Take my yoke upon you and*
> *learn from me, for I am gentle and humble in heart, and you*
> *will find rest for your souls."*
>
> ᗡ MATTHEW 11:28–29

> *"I will refresh the weary and satisfy the faint," says the LORD.*
>
> ᗡ JEREMIAH 31:25

> *Shout for joy, O heavens;*
> *rejoice, O earth;*
> *burst into song, O mountains!*
> *For the LORD comforts his people*
> *and will have compassion on his afflicted ones.*
>
> ᗡ ISAIAH 49:13

> *I will build them up and not tear them down; I will plant*
> *them and not uproot them. I will give them a heart to know*
> *me, that I am the LORD. They will be my people, and I will be*
> *their God.*
>
> ᗡ JEREMIAH 24:6–7

THIS ALWAYS
bothered me

God

is with us . . .

Should We Fret?

Fretting and a kitchen blender have a lot in common. With the push of a button the contents of a blender are whirled and swirled until they become a frothy mixture. In our lives, fretting gnaws away at us until our lives become a churned jumble. But God doesn't want us to live "blender-ized" lives.

> *Do not fret because of evil men*
> *or be envious of those who do wrong;*
> *for like the grass they will soon wither,*
> *like green plants they will soon die away.*
> *Trust in the LORD and do good.*
>
> ℭ PSALM 37:1–3

> *Be still before the LORD and wait patiently for him.*
>
> ℭ PSALM 37:7

> *God did not give us a spirit of timidity, but a spirit of power, of love and of self-discipline.*
>
> ℭ 2 TIMOTHY 1:7

Fretting easily leads to worry; worry casts a big shadow over small problems—a shadow that should never cross our lives.

Cast all your anxiety on God because he cares for you.

⌐ 1 PETER 5:7

Jesus said "Do not worry about your life, what you will eat; or about your body, what you will wear. Life is more than food, and the body more than clothes."

⌐ LUKE 12:22–23

Who of you by worrying can add a single hour to his life? And why do you worry about clothes? See how the lilies of the field grow. They do not labor or spin. Yet I tell you that not even Solomon in all his splendor was dressed like one of these. If that is how God clothes the grass of the field, which is here today and tomorrow is thrown into the fire, will he not much more clothe you, O you of little faith?

⌐ MATTHEW 6:27–30

When the outlook is not good, we should not fret. We need a change of perspective to realize that God sees tomorrow more clearly than we see yesterday. The future is completely in his hands!

When they heard that the LORD was concerned about them
and had seen their misery, they bowed down and worshiped.

C— EXODUS 4:31

"I am concerned for you and will look on you with favor,"
says the LORD.

C— EZEKIEL 36:9

Commit to the LORD whatever you do,
and your plans will succeed.

C— PROVERBS 16:3

The LORD gives strength to his people;
the LORD blesses his people with peace.

C— PSALM 29:11

Don't fret! Cheer up! Neither the sun, nor the Son, have gone out
of business. He is with us. A new day will dawn and the Lord will bring
himself to the center of our problems.

Blessed is the man who trusts in the LORD,
whose confidence is in him.
He will be like a tree planted by the water
that sends out its roots by the stream.
It does not fear when heat comes;
its leaves are always green.
It has no worries in a year of drought
and never fails to bear fruit.

C— JEREMIAH 17:7–8

Cast your cares on the LORD
and he will sustain you;
he will never let the righteous fall.

C— PSALM 55:22

Let us then approach the throne of grace with confidence, so that we may receive mercy and find grace to help us in our time of need.

                                ~ HEBREWS 4:16

The LORD is with you when you are with him. If you seek him, he will be found by you.

                          ~ 2 CHRONICLES 15:2

My flesh and my heart may fail,
but God is the strength of my heart
and my portion forever.

                                ~ PSALM 73:26

Be on your guard; stand firm in the faith; be men of courage; be strong.

                          ~ 1 CORINTHIANS 16:13

He who fears the LORD has a secure fortress.

                              ~ PROVERBS 14:26

Great peace have they who love God's law,
and nothing can make them stumble.

                            ~ PSALM 119:165

The LORD himself goes before you and will be with you; he will never leave you nor forsake you. Do not be afraid; do not be discouraged.

                        ~ DEUTERONOMY 31:8

God has said,

"Never will I leave you;
never will I forsake you."

So we say with confidence,

"The Lord is my helper; I will not be afraid.
What can man do to me?"

ⅆ HEBREWS 13:5–6

No one will be able to stand up against you all the days of
your life. I will be with you; I will never leave you nor for-
sake you," says the LORD.

ⅆ JOSHUA 1:5

Have I not commanded you? Be strong and courageous. Do
not be terrified; do not be discouraged, for the Lord your
God will be with you wherever you go.

ⅆ JOSHUA 1:9

Remember, fretting will only tie us in knots. Prayer is the only way to cut short our fretting—to cut those knots of worry and care and grant us God's peace instead.

Do not be anxious about anything, but in everything, by
prayer and petition, with thanksgiving, present your requests
to God. And the peace of God, which transcends all under-
standing, will guard your hearts and your minds in Christ
Jesus.

ⅆ PHILIPPIANS 4:6–7

AND I QUESTIONED THE
Lord about my dilemma

God
is with us . . .

When We Need Direction

When a transit strike brought our recently purchased business to a standstill, I found myself wondering if we had made the right decision to get into this new business. The choice had seemed to be the right one at the time, but now, I wasn't so sure. How was I supposed to sort out what we should do next? When we face questions of this kind, we need to get our arms around God's wisdom . . .

"I will instruct you and teach you in the way you should go;
I will counsel you and watch over you," says the LORD.

 ⌒ PSALM 32:8

Trust in the LORD *with all your heart*
and lean not on your own understanding;
in all your ways acknowledge him,
and he will make your paths straight.

 ⌒ PROVERBS 3:5–6

This is what the LORD *says—*
your Redeemer, the Holy One of Israel:
"I am the LORD *your God,*
who teaches you what is best for you,
who directs you in the way you should go."

 ⌒ ISAIAH 48:17

You discern my going out and my lying down;
you are familiar with all my ways, O LORD.

 ⌒ PSALM 139:3

The way of a fool seems right to him,
but a wise man listens to advice.

 ⌒ PROVERBS 12:15

*The L*ORD *will guide you always;*
he will satisfy your needs in a sun-scorched land
and will strengthen your frame.
You will be like a well-watered garden,
like a spring whose waters never fail.

ᗡ ISAIAH 58:11

*Show me your ways, O L*ORD,
teach me your paths;
guide me in your truth and teach me,
for you are God my Savior,
and my hope is in you all day long.

ᗡ PSALM 25:4–5

Many peoples will come and say,

*"Come, let us go up to the mountain of the L*ORD,
to the house of the God of Jacob.
He will teach us his ways,
so that we may walk in his paths."

ᗡ ISAIAH 2:3

*For the L*ORD *gives wisdom,*
and from his mouth come knowledge and understanding.

ᗡ PROVERBS 2:6

Whether you turn to the right or to the left, your ears will
hear a voice behind you, saying, "This is the way; walk in it."

ᗡ ISAIAH 30:21

God doesn't mind our questions when we come to him with a seeking heart. God is bigger than any question we can ask. And he often will give us the answers we seek in his Word.

> *Your word is a lamp to my feet*
> *and a light for my path.*

> ᝢ PSALM 119:105

> *These commands are a lamp,*
> *this teaching is a light,*
> *and the corrections of discipline*
> *are the way to life.*

> ᝢ PROVERBS 6:23

> *Do not let this Book of the Law depart from your mouth;*
> *meditate on it day and night, so that you may be careful to*
> *do everything written in it. Then you will be prosperous and*
> *successful.*

> ᝢ JOSHUA 1:8

> *Pay attention and listen to the sayings of the wise;*
> *apply your heart to what I teach,*
> *for it is pleasing when you keep them in your heart*
> *and have all of them ready on your lips.*
> *So that your trust may be in the LORD.*

> ᝢ PROVERBS 22:17–19

When we find ourselves questioning God's reason for allowing certain things to happen, we must stop, remember God's faithfulness and depend upon his grace. Whatever our questions, whatever our circumstances, God is still in control.

Since you are my rock and my fortress,
for the sake of your name lead and guide me, O LORD.

C~ PSALM 31:3

If the LORD delights in a man's way,
he makes his steps firm;
though he stumble, he will not fall,
for the LORD upholds him with his hand.

C~ PSALM 37:23–24

When we need direction we must trust that the Lord will take our faith, limited as it is, and make something of lasting value out of it. God has a plan for us. He cares about our dilemmas, hears our heartfelt cries and will answer us in ways that will astonish us and fill our hearts with songs of joy.

Let us acknowledge the LORD;
let us press on to acknowledge him.
As surely as the sun rises,
he will appear;
he will come to us like the winter rains,
like the spring rains that water the earth.

C~ HOSEA 6:3

For this God is our God for ever and ever;
he will be our guide even to the end.

C~ PSALM 48:14

"For I know the plans I have for you," declares the LORD,
"plans to prosper you and not to harm you, plans to give you
hope and a future."

C~ JEREMIAH 29:11

"LORD, YOU TOLD ME WHEN I decided to follow You. . ."

God
is with us . . .

In Our Decisions

It seems that sometimes all we do is make decisions. Purchases at the grocery store are easy, but life-changing decisions are more difficult. How can God help us?

The Lord says, "I guide you in the way of wisdom
and lead you along straight paths."

↶ Proverbs 4:11

Trust in the Lord with all your heart
and lean not on your own understanding;
in all your ways acknowledge him,
and he will make your paths straight.
Do not be wise in your own eyes.

↶ Proverbs 3:5–7

Do you not know?
Have you not heard?
The Lord is the everlasting God,
the Creator of the ends of the earth.
He will not grow tired or weary,
and his understanding no one can fathom.
He gives strength to the weary
and increases the power of the weak.

↶ Isaiah 40:28–29

The Lord gives wisdom,
and from his mouth come knowledge and understanding.

↶ Proverbs 2:6

Where then does wisdom come from?
Where does understanding dwell?
It is hidden from the eyes of every living thing,
concealed even from the birds of the air . . .
God understands the way to it
and he alone knows where it dwells.

↶ Job 28:20–21, 23

The decisions we need to make may be simple or they may be complex, but they should always be predicated on our decision to follow the Lord.

What does the LORD your God ask of you but to fear the LORD your God, to walk in all his ways, to love him, to serve the LORD your God with all your heart and with all your soul, and to observe the LORD's commands and decrees that I am giving you today for your own good?

      DEUTERONOMY 10:12–13

Fear the LORD and serve him faithfully with all your heart; consider what great things he has done for you.

      1 SAMUEL 12:24

Jesus said, "Whoever acknowledges me before men, I will also acknowledge him before my Father in heaven."

      MATTHEW 10:32

Choose . . . whom you will serve. As for me and my house, we will serve the LORD.

      JOSHUA 24:15

If anyone speaks, he should do it as one speaking the very words of God. If anyone serves, he should do it with the strength God provides, so that in all things God may be praised through Jesus Christ.

↪ 1 Peter 4:11

Keep the commandment to love the Lord *your God, to walk in all his ways, to obey his commands, to hold fast to him and to serve him with all your heart and all your soul.*

↪ Joshua 22:5

It is the LORD your God you must follow, and him you must revere. Keep his commands and obey him; serve him and hold fast to him.

⌒ DEUTERONOMY 13:4

When we decide to follow the Lord it means we must live our lives the way he wants us to, following his commands, yielded to his control.

Those who live according to the sinful nature have their minds set on what that nature desires; but those who live in accordance with the Spirit have their minds set on what the Spirit desires.

⌒ ROMANS 8:5

The one who sows to please his sinful nature, from that nature will reap destruction; the one who sows to please the Spirit, from the Spirit will reap eternal life.

⌒ GALATIANS 6:8

Forgetting what is behind and straining toward what is ahead, I press on toward the goal to win the prize for which God has called me heavenward in Christ Jesus.

⌒ PHILIPPIANS 3:13–14

The grace of God that brings salvation has appeared to all men. It teaches us to say "No" to ungodliness and worldly passions, and to live self-controlled, upright and godly lives in this present age.

⌒ TITUS 2:11–12

Make every effort to live in peace with all men and to be holy.

⌒ HEBREWS 12:14

Offer your bodies as living sacrifices, holy and pleasing to God—this is your spiritual act of worship. Do not conform any longer to the pattern of this world, but be transformed by the renewing of your mind.

ROMANS 12:1–2

What does the LORD your God ask of you but to fear the LORD your God, to walk in all his ways, to love him, to serve the LORD your God with all your heart and with all your soul.

DEUTERONOMY 10:12

Serve him with wholehearted devotion and with a willing mind, for the LORD searches every heart and understands every motive behind the thoughts.

1 CHRONICLES 28:9

Now that you have been set free from sin and have become slaves to God, the benefit you reap leads to holiness, and the result is eternal life.

ROMANS 6:22

Let us purify ourselves from everything that contaminates body and spirit, perfecting holiness out of reverence for God.

2 CORINTHIANS 7:1

Be holy in all you do; for it is written: "Be holy, because I am holy."

1 PETER 1:15–16

Pursue righteousness, godliness, faith, love, endurance and gentleness. Fight the good fight of the faith.

1 TIMOTHY 6:11–12

Just as you received Christ Jesus as Lord, continue to live in him, rooted and built up in him, strengthened in the faith as you were taught, and overflowing with thankfulness.

                                             ᶜ COLOSSIANS 2:6–7

Do not turn away from the LORD, but serve the LORD with all your heart.

                                               ᶜ 1 SAMUEL 12:20

*Let your eyes look straight ahead,
fix your gaze directly before you.
Make level paths for your feet
and take only ways that are firm.*

                                             ᶜ PROVERBS 4:25–26

We must pay more careful attention, therefore, to what we have heard, so that we do not drift away.

                                             ᶜ HEBREWS 2:1

Let us hold unswervingly to the hope we profess, for he who promised is faithful.

                                             ᶜ HEBREWS 10:23

Since we are surrounded by such a great cloud of witnesses, let us throw off everything that hinders and the sin that so easily entangles, and let us run with perseverance the race marked out for us.

                                             ᶜ HEBREWS 12:1

LORD, who may dwell in your sanctuary?
Who may live on your holy hill?
He whose walk is blameless
and who does what is righteous,
who speaks the truth from his heart.

                                   PSALM 15:1–2

He has showed you, O man, what is good.
And what does the LORD require of you?
To act justly and to love mercy
and to walk humbly with your God.

                                   MICAH 6:8

We all need God's divine power from day to day to follow in his footsteps—to learn the eternal, upside-down, inside-out values of God's kingdom so that we may make decisions based on his character and ultimately share in his glory.

"YOU WOULD WALK AND
talk with me all the way."

God

is with us . . .

As Our Guide

I saw two children walking together today, happily exchanging words and glances, laughing aloud at shared jokes. They didn't worry about the cracks in the sidewalk or the bumps in the road, but rather skipped along over them. God wants our walk with him to be just like that—enjoying his company, sharing together and crossing the rough places on our journey home without the slightest care.

If we claim to have fellowship with him yet walk in the darkness, we lie and do not live by the truth. But if we walk in the light, as he is in the light, we have fellowship with one another, and the blood of Jesus, his Son, purifies us from all sin.

1 JOHN 1:6–7

Whoever claims to live in him must walk as Jesus did.

            ᴄ~ 1 JOHN 2:6

Righteousness goes before him
and prepares the way for his steps.

            ᴄ~ PSALM 85:13

O LORD, . . . I have walked before you faithfully and with
wholehearted devotion and have done what is good in your eyes.

            ᴄ~ 2 KINGS 20:3

You have delivered me from death
and my feet from stumbling,
that I may walk before God in the light of life.

        ᴄ~ Psalm 56:13

Blessed are those who have learned to acclaim you,
who walk in the light of your presence, O Lord.

        ᴄ~ Psalm 89:15

The ways of the Lord are right;
the righteous walk in them,
but the rebellious stumble in them.

        ᴄ~ Hosea 14:9

Many times along our life-walk the path becomes obscure. We need someone to help show us the way. That someone is God.

The Lord will guide you always;
he will satisfy your needs in a sun-scorched land
and will strengthen your frame.
You will be like a well-watered garden,
like a spring whose waters never fail.

        ᴄ~ Isaiah 58:11

God guides the humble in what is right
and teaches them his way.

        ᴄ~ Psalm 25:9

O Lord since you are my rock and my fortress,
for the sake of your name lead and guide me.

        ᴄ~ Psalm 31:3

O Lord, you guide me with your counsel.

        ᴄ~ Psalm 73:24

*This is what the L*ORD *says—*
your Redeemer, the Holy One of Israel:
*"I am the L*ORD *your God,*
who teaches you what is best for you,
who directs you in the way you should go."

⌐ ISAIAH 48:17

*Show me your ways, O L*ORD,
teach me your paths;
guide me in your truth and teach me,
for you are God my Savior,
and my hope is in you all day long.

⌐ PSALM 25:4–5

God will teach us his ways,
so that we may walk in his paths.

⌐ ISAIAH 2:3

If any of you lacks wisdom, he should ask God, who gives generously to all without finding fault, and it will be given to him.

                                    JAMES 1:5

Teach me your way, O LORD;
lead me in a straight path.

                                    PSALM 27:11

Lead me, O LORD, in your righteousness . . .
make straight your way before me.

                                    PSALM 5:8

Trust in the LORD with all your heart
and lean not on your own understanding;
in all your ways acknowledge him,
and he will make your paths straight.

                                    PROVERBS 3:5–6

Show me the way I should go,
for to you I lift up my soul.

                                    PSALM 143:8

God who has compassion on them will guide them
and lead them beside springs of water.

                                    ISAIAH 49:10

Teach me to do your will,
for you are my God;
may your good Spirit
lead me on level ground.

                                    PSALM 143:10

God's Word becomes our road map for our daily walk with the Savior.

Your word is a lamp to my feet
and a light for my path, O LORD.

                     PSALM 119:105

These commands are a lamp,
this teaching is a light,
and the corrections of discipline
are the way to life.

                     PROVERBS 6:23

His Word reminds us of his power, his provision and his sovereignty.

"For I know the plans I have for you," declares the LORD,
"plans to prosper you and not to harm you, plans to give you
hope and a future."

                     JEREMIAH 29:11

Commit to the Lord whatever you do,
and your plans will succeed.

                     PROVERBS 16:3

My flesh and my heart may fail,
but God is the strength of my heart
and my portion forever.

                     PSALM 73:26

If the Lord delights in a man's way,
he makes his steps firm;
though he stumble, he will not fall,
for the Lord upholds him with his hand.

                                Psalm 37:23–24

His Word reminds us of his love.

This I call to mind
and therefore I have hope:
Because of the Lord's great love we are not consumed,
for his compassions never fail.
They are new every morning;
great is your faithfulness.

                             Lamentations 3:21–23

The Lord will fulfill his purpose for me;
your love, O Lord, endures forever.

                                   Psalm 138:8

How great is the love the Father has lavished on us, that we
should be called children of God!

                                   1 John 3:1

Let's enjoy the time with God as he walks and talks with us each day, wherever we are, for "this God is our God for ever and ever; he will be our guide even to the end" (Psalm 48:14).

"Be still, and know that I am God;
I will be exalted among the nations,
I will be exalted in the earth."
The Lord Almighty is with us;
the God of Jacob is our fortress.

                                Psalm 46:10–11

"BUT I'M AWARE THAT DURING THE MOST TROUBLESOME TIMES OF MY LIFE *there is only one set of footprints.*"

God
is with us . . .

In Our Difficulties

Ruts and potholes. Shadows and deep darkness. The journey of life can sometimes be very troubling. We stumble and have difficulty following in God's footsteps. We are fearful of the unknown. But God's Word reminds us to trust, to believe, to hope.

Be strong and take heart,
all you who hope in the LORD.

                                                 PSALM 31:24

Now, LORD, what do I look for?
My hope is in you.

                                                 PSALM 39:7

Why are you downcast, O my soul?
Why so disturbed within me?
Put your hope in God,
for I will yet praise him,
my Savior and my God.

                                             PSALM 43:5–6

You have been my hope, O Sovereign LORD,
my confidence since my youth.

                                               PSALM 71:5

Put your hope in the LORD,
for with the LORD is unfailing love
and with him is full redemption.

                                           PSALM 130:7

Blessed is the man who trusts in the LORD,
whose confidence is in him.

                                             JEREMIAH 17:7

Blessed is he whose help is the God of Jacob,
whose hope is in the LORD his God,
the Maker of heaven and earth,
the sea, and everything in them—
the LORD, who remains faithful forever.

PSALM 146:5–6

This I call to mind and therefore I have hope:
Because of the LORD's great love we are not consumed,
for his compassions never fail.

∽ LAMENTATIONS 3:21–22

The LORD is good to those whose hope is in him,
to the one who seeks him.

∽ LAMENTATIONS 3:25

When I am afraid,
I will trust in you.
In God, whose word I praise,
in God I trust; I will not be afraid.
What can mortal man do to me?

∽ PSALM 56:3–4

As for me, I watch in hope for the LORD,
I wait for God my Savior;
my God will hear me.

∽ MICAH 7:7

We all go through troubling times, but we must never doubt God's presence with us.

Jesus said, "Surely I am with you always, to the very end of the age."

           MATTHEW 28:20

Do not fear, for I am with you;
do not be dismayed, for I am your God.
I will strengthen you and help you;
I will uphold you with my righteous right hand.

           ISAIAH 41:10

The LORD your God is a merciful God; he will not abandon or destroy you.

           DEUTERONOMY 4:31

Those who know your name will trust in you,
for you, LORD, have never forsaken those who seek you.

           PSALM 9:10

Where can I go from your Spirit?
Where can I flee from God's presence?
If I go up to the heavens, you are there;
if I make my bed in the depths, you are there.
If I rise on the wings of the dawn,
if I settle on the far side of the sea,
even there your hand will guide me,
your right hand will hold me fast.

                        PSALM 139:7–10

God will never let us down. He promises us his strength, his peace, his comfort and his presence. All we need to do is depend on him, for we can never break God's promises by leaning on them.

Do not be afraid. Stand firm and you will see the deliverance the LORD will bring you today. . . . The LORD will fight for you; you need only to be still.

                        EXODUS 14:13–14

The eternal God is your refuge,
and underneath are the everlasting arms.

                        DEUTERONOMY 33:27

"For I know the plans I have for you," declares the LORD,
"plans to prosper you and not to harm you, plans to give you
hope and a future."

                        JEREMIAH 29:11

The LORD longs to be gracious to you;
he rises to show you compassion.

                        ISAIAH 30:18

I will build them up and not tear them down; I will plant them and not uproot them. I will give them a heart to know me, that I am the L<small>ORD</small>. They will be my people, and I will be their God, for they will return to me with all their heart.

~ J<small>EREMIAH</small> 24:6–7

Jesus said, "In this world you will have trouble. But take heart! I have overcome the world."

~ J<small>OHN</small> 16:33

We know that in all things God works for the good of those who love him, who have been called according to his purpose.

~ R<small>OMANS</small> 8:28

"Call upon me in the day of trouble;
I will deliver you, and you will honor me."

~ P<small>SALM</small> 50:15

The L<small>ORD</small> is a refuge for the oppressed,
a stronghold in times of trouble.
Those who know your name will trust in you,
for you, L<small>ORD</small>, have never forsaken those who seek you.

~ P<small>SALM</small> 9:9–10

Cast your cares on the L<small>ORD</small>
and he will sustain you;
he will never let the righteous fall.

~ P<small>SALM</small> 55:22

If the LORD delights in a man's way,
he makes his steps firm;
though he stumble, he will not fall,
for the LORD upholds him with his hand.

           ◌ PSALM 37:23–24

The LORD is good,
a refuge in times of trouble.
He cares for those who trust in him.

           ◌ NAHUM 1:7

Who shall separate us from the love of Christ? Shall trouble or
hardship or persecution or famine or nakedness or danger or
sword . . . No, in all these things we are more than conquerors
through him who loved us.

           ◌ ROMANS 8:35, 37

Those things we consider difficulties are often God's opportunities for our greater blessing. We must trust, believe, hope and continue to walk the path he has laid before us.

May our Lord Jesus Christ himself and God our Father, who
loved us and by his grace gave us eternal encouragement and
good hope, encourage your hearts and strengthen you in every
good deed and word.

           ◌ 2 THESSALONIANS 2:16–17

"I JUST DON'T UNDERSTAND WHY,
when I needed You the most, You leave me."

God

is with us . . .

In Our Confusion

Many things in life cannot be explained: the death of an infant, the loss of a job, the rebellion of a child, the desertion by a loved one, or any number of circumstances beyond our control. Have you ever wondered, *Why did this have to happen?* God can help us with those "Why?" questions.

David questioned God,

> *"Has his unfailing love vanished forever?*
> *Has his promise failed for all time?*
> *Has God forgotten to be merciful?*
> *Has he in anger withheld his compassion?"*
>
> C~ PSALM 77:8–9

> *We know that in all things God works for the good of those who love him, who have been called according to his purpose.*
>
> C~ ROMANS 8:28

> *There is a time for everything*
> *and a season for every activity under heaven.*
>
> C~ ECCLESIASTES 3:1

> *When times are good, be happy;*
> *but when times are bad, consider:*
> *God has made the one*
> *as well as the other.*
>
> C~ ECCLESIASTES 7:14

"My thoughts are not your thoughts,
neither are your ways my ways,"
    declares the LORD.
"As the heavens are higher than the earth,
so are my ways higher than your ways
and my thoughts than your thoughts."

    ᴄ ISAIAH 55:8–9

When faced with bewildering circumstances we are tempted to ask "Why?" But a better question to ask is "What . . . what do you have in mind now, Lord?"

"Call to me and I will answer you and tell you great and
unsearchable things you do not know," says the LORD.

    ᴄ JEREMIAH 33:3

Cast your cares on the LORD
and he will sustain you;
he will never let the righteous fall.

    ᴄ PSALM 55:22

Let us acknowledge the LORD;
let us press on to acknowledge him.
As surely as the sun rises,
he will appear;
he will come to us like the winter rains,
like the spring rains that water the earth.

    ᴄ HOSEA 6:3

O LORD, it was good for me to be afflicted
so that I might learn your decrees.

C~ PSALM 119:71

Though it may sometimes seem that things are out of control, we can take comfort in God's enduring promises and constant presence.

A righteous man may have many troubles,
but the LORD delivers him from them all.

C~ PSALM 34:19

"I will make an everlasting covenant with them: I will never
stop doing good to them," says the LORD.

C~ JEREMIAH 32:40

Your love, O LORD, endures forever.

C~ PSALM 138:8

Be strong and courageous. Do not be terrified; do not be dis-
couraged, for the LORD your God will be with you wherever
you go.

C~ JOSHUA 1:9

I the LORD do not change.

C~ MALACHI 3:6

You, O Lord, are a compassionate and gracious God,
slow to anger, abounding in love and faithfulness.

C~ PSALM 86:15

His mercy extends to those who fear him, from generation to generation.

⁓ LUKE 1:50

O LORD, you are my hiding place;
you will protect me from trouble
and surround me with songs of deliverance.

⁓ PSALM 32:7

Who is a God like you,
who pardons sin and forgives the transgression
of the remnant of his inheritance?
You do not stay angry forever
but delight to show mercy.
You will again have compassion on us.

⁓ MICAH 7:18–19

This I call to mind
and therefore I have hope:
Because of the LORD's great love we are not consumed,
for his compassions never fail.
They are new every morning;
great is your faithfulness.

⁓ LAMENTATIONS 3:21–23

Let us hold unswervingly to the hope we profess, for God who promised is faithful.

⁓ HEBREWS 10:23

God, who has called you into fellowship with his Son Jesus Christ our Lord, is faithful.

☙ 1 CORINTHIANS 1:9

Commit to the LORD whatever you do, and your plans will succeed.

☙ PROVERBS 16:3

The LORD is good to those whose hope is in him, to the one who seeks him.

☙ LAMENTATIONS 3:25

Jesus said, "Blessed are you who hunger now, for you will be satisfied. Blessed are you who weep now, for you will laugh."

☙ LUKE 6:21

Put away all doubts. Cast out all confusion. Stand firm in the work of the Lord and find a renewed faith following in his footsteps.

The LORD is my strength and my shield; my heart trusts in him, and I am helped.

My heart leaps for joy and I will give thanks to him.

☙ PSALM 28:7

HE WHISPERED,
"My precious child, . . ."

147

God

is with us . . .

As Our Loving Father

The Creator of the universe calls me his child—what a blessing!
What a privilege! What a responsibility!

The LORD disciplines those he loves,
as a father the son he delights in.

℃ PROVERBS 3:12

"I will be a Father to you,
and you will be my sons and daughters,"
says the Lord Almighty.

℃ 2 CORINTHIANS 6:18

Endure hardship as discipline; God is treating you as sons.
For what son is not disciplined by his father?

℃ HEBREWS 12:7

David declared, "You are my Father,
my God, the Rock my Savior."

PSALM 89:26

You, O LORD, are our Father,
our Redeemer from of old is your name.

ISAIAH 63:16

To us a child is born,
to us a son is given,
and the government will be on his shoulders.
And he will be called . . .
Everlasting Father.

ISAIAH 9:6

O LORD, you are our Father.
We are the clay, you are the potter;
we are all the work of your hand.

           ℂ ISAIAH 64:8

How great is the love the Father has lavished on us, that we
should be called children of God!

           ℂ 1 JOHN 3:1

You did not receive a spirit that makes you a slave again to
fear, but you received the Spirit of sonship. And by him we
cry, "Abba, Father."

           ℂ ROMANS 8:15

For us there is but one God, the Father, from whom all
things came and for whom we live; and there is but one
Lord, Jesus Christ, through whom all things came and
through whom we live.

           ℂ 1 CORINTHIANS 8:6

There is one body and one Spirit—just as you were called
to one hope when you were called—one Lord, one faith,
one baptism; one God and Father of all, who is over all and
through all and in all.

           ℂ EPHESIANS 4:4–6

As children of God we can trust that our Father will provide for us.

Jesus said, "Your Father knows what you need before you ask him."

CROP MATTHEW 6:8

Jesus said, "Which of you fathers, if your son asks for a fish, will give him a snake instead? Or if he asks for an egg, will give him a scorpion? If you then, though you are evil, know how to give good gifts to your children, how much more will your Father in heaven give the Holy Spirit to those who ask him!"

LUKE 11:11–13

As God's children, our Father knows us by name and bestows on us certain rights, privileges and responsibilities.

I, the LORD, have called you in righteousness;
I will take hold of your hand.
I will keep you and will make you
to be a covenant for the people
and a light for the Gentiles.

ISAIAH 42:6

Before I was born the LORD called me;
from my birth he has made mention of my name.

ISAIAH 49:1

This is what the LORD says . . .
he who formed you. . . .
"Fear not, for I have redeemed you;
I have summoned you by name; you are mine."

ᴄ— ISAIAH 43:1

"I will pour out my Spirit on your offspring,
and my blessing on your descendants.
They will spring up like grass in a meadow,
like poplar trees by flowing streams.
One will say, 'I belong to the LORD;'
another will call himself by the name of Jacob;
still another will write on his hand, 'The LORD's.'"

ᴄ— ISAIAH 44:3–5

Our loving Father cares for us as a shepherd cares for his sheep. And we, his children, need to listen carefully to his voice and obey.

Jesus said, "The sheep listen to his voice. He calls his own
sheep by name and leads them out. When he has brought out
all his own, he goes on ahead of them, and his sheep follow
him because they know his voice."

ᴄ— JOHN 10:3–4

Jesus said, "I am the good shepherd; I know my sheep and my
sheep know me—just as the Father knows me and I know the
Father—and I lay down my life for the sheep."

ᴄ— JOHN 10:14–15

"I LOVE YOU AND WILL
NEVER LEAVE YOU

never, ever, during your trials and testings."

God

is with us . . .

Always!

We often make promises we can't keep. God isn't like that. God is faithful and trustworthy. When God promises never to leave us, he means just what he says. He's not going anywhere!

God has said,

> *"Never will I leave you;*
> *never will I forsake you."*

C⁓ HEBREWS 13:5

> *The LORD himself goes before you and will be with you; he will never leave you nor forsake you. Do not be afraid; do not be discouraged.*

C⁓ DEUTERONOMY 31:8

"No one will be able to stand up against you all the days of your life. As I was with Moses, so I will be with you; I will never leave you nor forsake you."

⇛ JOSHUA 1:5

Jesus said, "Surely I am with you always, to the very end of the age."

⇛ MATTHEW 28:20

"He will call upon me, and I will answer him;
I will be with him in trouble," says the LORD.

⇛ PSALM 91:15

Do not fear, for I am with you;
do not be dismayed, for I am your God.
I will strengthen you and help you;
I will uphold you with my righteous right hand.

⇛ ISAIAH 41:10

I am convinced that neither death nor life, neither angels nor demons, neither the present nor the future, nor any powers, neither height nor depth, nor anything else in all creation, will be able to separate us from the love of God that is in Christ Jesus our Lord.

⇛ ROMANS 8:38–39

Those who know your name will trust in you,
for you, LORD, have never forsaken those who seek you.

⇛ PSALM 9:10

*Be strong and courageous. Do not be afraid or terrified
. . . for the L*ORD *your God goes with you; he will never
leave you nor forsake you.*

꿈 DEUTERONOMY 31:6

*Jesus said, "Here I am! I stand at the door and knock. If
anyone hears my voice and opens the door, I will come in
and eat with him, and he with me."*

꿈 REVELATION 3:20

*"Though the mountains be shaken
and the hills be removed,
yet my unfailing love for you will not be shaken
nor my covenant of peace be removed,"
says the L*ORD, *who has compassion on you.*

꿈 ISAIAH 54:10

*Be strong and courageous. Do not be terrified; do not
be discouraged, for the L*ORD *your God will be with you
wherever you go.*

꿈 JOSHUA 1:9

*Where can I go from your Spirit?
Where can I flee from God's presence?
If I go up to the heavens, you are there;
if I make my bed in the depths, you are there.
If I rise on the wings of the dawn,
if I settle on the far side of the sea,
even there your hand will guide me,
your right hand will hold me fast.*

꿈 PSALM 139:7–10

The LORD watches over you—
the LORD is your shade at your right hand;
the sun will not harm you by day,
nor the moon by night.
The LORD will keep you from all harm—
he will watch over your life;
the LORD will watch over your coming and going
both now and forevermore.

 ◠ PSALM 121:5–8

When it seems that life is whirling out of control, we can take comfort in God's sovereignty and power. He has everything under control. And he will work his will in every circumstance.

Commit your way to the LORD;
trust in him and he will do this:
He will make your righteousness shine like the dawn,
the justice of your cause like the noonday sun.

 ◠ PSALM 37:5–6

Commit to the LORD whatever you do,
and your plans will succeed.

 ◠ PROVERBS 16:3

Many are the plans in a man's heart,
but it is the LORD's purpose that prevails.

 ◠ PROVERBS 19:21

Cast all your anxiety on God because he cares for you.

 ◠ 1 PETER 5:7

Do not be anxious about anything, but in everything, by prayer and petition, with thanksgiving, present your requests to God. And the peace of God, which transcends all understanding, will guard your hearts and your minds in Christ Jesus.

ᴄ Philippians 4:6–7

The Lord Almighty has purposed, and who can thwart him? His hand is stretched out, and who can turn it back?

ᴄ Isaiah 14:27

"I make known the end from the beginning,
from ancient times, what is still to come.
I say: My purpose will stand,
and I will do all that I please."

ᴄ Isaiah 46:10

Jesus said, "Look at the birds of the air; they do not sow or reap or store away in barns, and yet your heavenly Father feeds them. Are you not much more valuable than they? Who of you by worrying can add a single hour to his life?"

ᴄ Matthew 6:26–27

I know that you can do all things;
no plan of yours can be thwarted, O Lord.

ᴄ Job 42:2

The LORD is with you when you are with him. If you seek him, he will be found by you.

                                 2 CHRONICLES 15:2

I know that everything God does will endure forever; nothing can be added to it and nothing taken from it. God does it so that men will revere him.

                                  ECCLESIASTES 3:14

The LORD gives strength to his people;
the LORD blesses his people with peace.

                                  PSALM 29:11

O LORD, great peace have they who love your law,
and nothing can make them stumble.

                                  PSALM 119:165

My flesh and my heart may fail,
but God is the strength of my heart
and my portion forever.

                                  PSALM 73:26

Those who trust in the LORD are like Mount Zion,
which cannot be shaken but endures forever.

                                  PSALM 125:1

Whenever we hit rock-bottom, we can be assured of God's love and care. His encouragement breathes new possibilities into impossible circumstances.

In you, O LORD, I have taken refuge;
let me never be put to shame;
deliver me in your righteousness.

PSALM 31:1

Let us then approach the throne of grace with confidence, so
that we may receive mercy and find grace to help us in our
time of need.

HEBREWS 4:16

The LORD is with me; I will not be afraid.

PSALM 118:6

Taste and see that the LORD is good;
blessed is the man who takes refuge in him.

PSALM 34:8

Cast your cares on the LORD
and he will sustain you;
he will never let the righteous fall.

PSALM 55:22

So we say with confidence,

"The Lord is my helper; I will not be afraid.
What can man do to me?"

HEBREWS 13:6

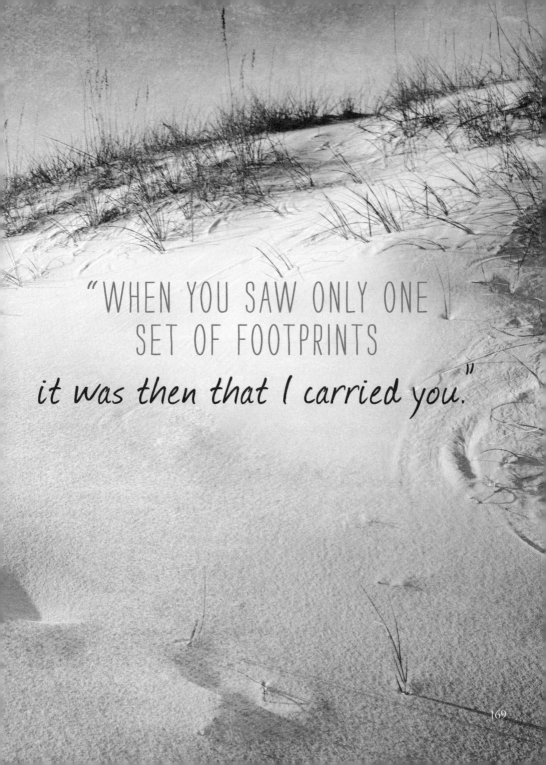

"WHEN YOU SAW ONLY ONE
SET OF FOOTPRINTS
it was then that I carried you."

God

is with us . . .

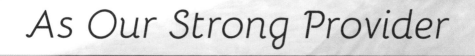

As Our Strong Provider

Our problems may seem overwhelming, but God's power is stronger than any obstacle we may face.

> *I am the LORD, the God of all mankind. Is anything too hard for me?*
>
> ⌒ JEREMIAH 32:27

> *"There is no god besides me.*
> *I put to death and I bring to life,*
> *I have wounded and I will heal,*
> *and no one can deliver out of my hand."*
>
> ⌒ DEUTERONOMY 32:39

> *God does as he pleases*
> *with the powers of heaven*
> *and the peoples of the earth.*
> *No one can hold back his hand*
> *or say to him: "What have you done?"*
>
> ⌒ DANIEL 4:35

> *You are the ruler of all things.*
> *In your hands are strength and power*
> *to exalt and give strength to all.*
> *Now, our God, we give you thanks,*
> *and praise your glorious name.*
>
> ⌒ 1 CHRONICLES 29:12–13

> *All that we have accomplished*
> *you have done for us, O LORD.*
>
> ⌒ ISAIAH 26:12

Not that we are competent in ourselves to claim anything for ourselves, but our competence comes from God.

         2 CORINTHIANS 3:5

Jesus said, "With God all things are possible."

         MATTHEW 19:26

The LORD is slow to anger and great in power . . .
His way is in the whirlwind and the storm,
and clouds are the dust of his feet.

         NAHUM 1:3

I can do everything through Christ who gives me strength.

         PHILIPPIANS 4:13

Be strong in the Lord and in his mighty power.

C~ EPHESIANS 6:10

The eternal God is your refuge,
and underneath are the everlasting arms.

C~ DEUTERONOMY 33:27

The LORD gives strength to his people;
the LORD blesses his people with peace.

C~ PSALM 29:11

Jesus said, "My grace is sufficient for you, for my power is
made perfect in weakness."

C~ 2 CORINTHIANS 12:9

The LORD is the strength of his people,
a fortress of salvation for his anointed one.

C~ PSALM 28:8

So do not fear, for I am with you;
do not be dismayed, for I am your God.
I will strengthen you and help you;
I will uphold you with my righteous right hand.

⌒ ISAIAH 41:10

In the LORD alone
are righteousness and strength.

⌒ ISAIAH 45:24

"I will strengthen them in the LORD
and in his name they will walk,"
      declares the LORD.

⌒ ZECHARIAH 10:12

"I will refresh the weary and satisfy the faint," says the LORD.

⌒ JEREMIAH 31:25

He gives strength to the weary
and increases the power of the weak.
Even youths grow tired and weary,
and young men stumble and fall;
but those who hope in the LORD
will renew their strength.
They will soar on wings like eagles;
they will run and not grow weary,
they will walk and not be faint.

ISAIAH 40:29–31

Since God is our strong Provider, we can be assured that he is in control of every aspect of our lives. He will prepare the way before us. He will never leave us. And he will provide for our every need.

Those who know your name will trust in you,
for you, LORD, have never forsaken those who seek you.

            C~ PSALM 9:10

My God will meet all your needs according to his glorious
riches in Christ Jesus.

            C~ PHILIPPIANS 4:19

No eye has seen,
no ear has heard,
no mind has conceived
what God has prepared for those who love him.

            C~ 1 CORINTHIANS 2:9

Jesus said, "Come to me, all you who are weary and burdened, and I will give you rest."

                                         C MATTHEW 11:28

"Before they call I will answer;
while they are still speaking I will hear,"
    declares the LORD.

                                         C ISAIAH 65:24

Jesus said, "If you believe, you will receive whatever you ask for in prayer."

                                       C MATTHEW 21:22

Taste and see that the LORD is good;
blessed is the man who takes refuge in him.

                                       C PSALM 34:8

O LORD Almighty,
blessed is the man who trusts in you.

PSALM 84:12

Those who trust in the LORD are like Mount Zion,
which cannot be shaken but endures forever.

PSALM 125:1

Blessed is he whose help is the God of Jacob,
whose hope is in the LORD his God.

PSALM 146:5

He who did not spare his own Son, but gave him up for us
all—how will he not also, along with him, graciously give us
all things?

ROMANS 8:32

Jesus said, "Whoever drinks the water I give him will never
thirst. Indeed, the water I give him will become in him a
spring of water welling up to eternal life."

JOHN 4:14

Praise be to the Lord, to God our Savior,
who daily bears our burdens.

PSALM 68:19

You will keep in perfect peace
him whose mind is steadfast,
because he trusts in you, O LORD.

ISAIAH 26:3

But blessed is the man who trusts in the LORD,
whose confidence is in him.
He will be like a tree planted by the water
that sends out its roots by the stream.
It does not fear when heat comes;
its leaves are always green.
It has no worries in a year of drought
and never fails to bear fruit.

⌒ JEREMIAH 17:7–8

The LORD longs to be gracious to you;
he rises to show you compassion.
For the LORD is a God of justice.
Blessed are all who wait for him!

⌒ ISAIAH 30:18

Trust in the LORD with all your heart
and lean not on your own understanding.

⌒ PROVERBS 3:5

He who trusts in the LORD will prosper.

⌒ PROVERBS 28:25

As the Scripture says,

"Anyone who trusts in Christ will never be put to shame."

⌒ ROMANS 10:11

Be strong and take heart,
all you who hope in the LORD.

C~ PSALM 31:24

"When you pass through the waters,
I will be with you;
and when you pass through the rivers,
they will not sweep over you.
When you walk through the fire,
you will not be burned;
the flames will not set you ablaze."

C~ ISAIAH 43:2

Our God is strong enough to carry us, but also gentle enough to enfold us in his loving embrace.

God tends his flock like a shepherd:
He gathers the lambs in his arms
and carries them close to his heart;
he gently leads those that have young.

C~ ISAIAH 40:11

God will command his angels concerning you
to guard you in all your ways;
they will lift you up in their hands,
so that you will not strike your foot against a stone.

C~ PSALM 91:11–12

When have you needed
God most in your life?

_____

_____

_____

_____

_____

_____

_____

_____

_____

_____

_____

_____

_____

_____

When have you felt alone with your burdens?

When have you felt God carrying you?

_____

_____

_____

_____

_____

_____

_____

_____

_____

_____

_____

_____

_____